AF228557

DETROIT PISTONS

BY BRIAN HOWELL

SportsZone

An Imprint of Abdo Publishing
abdobooks.com

abdobooks.com

Published by Abdo Publishing, a division of ABDO, PO Box 398166, Minneapolis, Minnesota 55439. Copyright © 2023 by Abdo Consulting Group, Inc. International copyrights reserved in all countries. No part of this book may be reproduced in any form without written permission from the publisher. SportsZone™ is a trademark and logo of Abdo Publishing.

Printed in China.
052022
092022

Cover Photo: Nic Antaya/Getty Images Sport/Getty Images
Interior Photos: Melinda Nagy/Shutterstock Images, 1; Ezra Shaw/Getty Images Sport/ Getty Images, 4; Michael Conroy/AP Images, 7, 39; Tom Pidgeon/Getty Images Sport/ Getty Images, 8; Elsa/Getty Images Sport/Getty Images, 10; Jed Jacobsohn/Getty Images Sport/Getty Images, 13; Denver Post/Getty Images, 14; Focus on Sport/Getty Images, 17, 19; Doug Pizac/AP Images, 21; Jason Miller/Getty Images Sport/Getty Images, 23; Focus on Sport/Getty Images Sport/Getty Images, 24, 37; AP Images, 26; Bob Galbraith/ AP Images, 29; Jack Smith/AP Images, 30; Duane Burleson/AP Images, 32, 36; Nic Antaya/ Getty Images Sport/Getty Images, 33; Diamond Images/Getty Images, 34; Mary Altaffer/ AP Images, 41

Editor: Charlie Beattie
Series Designer: Joshua Olson

Library of Congress Control Number: 2021952317

Publisher's Cataloging-in-Publication Data

Names: Howell, Brian, author.
Title: Detroit Pistons / by Brian Howell
Description: Minneapolis, Minnesota: Abdo Publishing, 2023 | Series: Inside the NBA | Includes online resources and index.
Identifiers: ISBN 9781532198267 (lib. bdg.) | ISBN 9781098271916 (ebook)
Subjects: LCSH: Detroit Pistons (Basketball team)--Juvenile literature. | Basketball--Juvenile literature. | Professional sports--Juvenile literature. | Sports franchises--Juvenile literature.
Classification: DDC 796.32364--dc23

TABLE OF CONTENTS

AN UPSET FOR ALL TIME

More than 22,000 fans at the Palace of Auburn Hills erupted as Detroit Pistons point guard Chauncey Billups threw the ball high in the air. The Pistons had just defeated the Indiana Pacers 69–65 in Game 6 of the 2004 Eastern Conference finals. For the first time in 14 years, Detroit was headed back to the National Basketball Association (NBA) Finals.

It was a lively scene. And many NBA observers predicted that this was all the celebrating that Detroit would get to do that year. The Pistons were on their way to a championship series no expert thought they had a chance to win.

LUNCH-PAIL PISTONS

A year earlier, Detroit had reached the East finals as the conference's top seed. But the Pistons were blown away in a four-game sweep by the New Jersey Nets. Detroit general

Richard Hamilton's 17.6 points per game led a balanced Pistons attack in 2003–04.

manager Joe Dumars knew a change was needed to win a title. And Dumars was an expert on the subject. When Detroit had won its only NBA championships in 1989 and 1990, he was one of the Pistons' star players.

After that 2003 loss to the Nets, Dumars decided to try a new head coach. He let Rick Carlisle go, even though Carlisle had led Detroit to back-to-back 50–32 records. In his place, Dumars hired Larry Brown. The veteran Brown had been a professional and college coach since 1972. He had been successful, but he had never won an NBA title.

The team Brown inherited was a motley group of players. Billups was on his fifth NBA team. High-scoring shooting guard Richard "Rip" Hamilton had started his career with the Washington Wizards. Center Ben Wallace was an unknown role player until he got to Detroit in 2000. But he had become one of the league's best rebounders and shot blockers. Second-year small forward Tayshaun Prince was a gangly, 6-foot-9-inch, 212-pound collection of long arms and legs.

Under Brown the Pistons had a season of highs and lows. A stretch of seven losses in nine December games left Detroit just 16–13. The Pistons then rattled off a franchise-record-tying 13 straight wins, only to lose 11 of their next 16 games.

Dumars decided it was time to bring in more help. Forward Rasheed Wallace was his next target. Wallace was highly talented but combustible. He was known for arguing with

Hamilton, *right*, and center Ben Wallace, *left*, celebrate late in Game 5 of the 2004 NBA Finals.

referees and collecting technical fouls. He'd also had run-ins with teammates in previous stops. But in Detroit he fit right in. The Pistons rolled through the rest of the regular season by working together and playing historically good defense. In the playoffs they brushed off the Milwaukee Bucks before getting revenge on New Jersey in a seven-game series. Now the win over Indiana had them close to a title. There was just one huge problem.

UNDERDOGS

Ben Wallace was named the NBA's Defensive Player of the Year in 2003–04.

The Los Angeles Lakers were the NBA's dominant team in the early 2000s. Entering the 2003–04 season, they had won three of the last four NBA titles. They boasted superstars like guard Kobe Bryant and center Shaquille O'Neal. In the offseason, they had signed two future Hall of Famers in point guard Gary Payton and power forward Karl Malone. Their coach, Phil Jackson, was a nine-time NBA champion. And they had just cruised through the playoffs, beating the defending champion San Antonio Spurs along the way.

No one gave the Pistons a chance. Even in Detroit one of the local papers described the Pistons' chances of winning as "a crumpled lottery ticket." For many observers, the only

question was how many games
the Lakers would need to brush
Detroit aside.

However, the Pistons believed
in themselves. The team leaned
on defense. During the year,
Detroit had set a record by
holding five straight opponents
under 70 points in a game. That
kind of effort was on display
in Game 1 in Los Angeles.
The Pistons trailed by one at
halftime, but they shut down the
Lakers in the second half of a
surprise 87–75 win.

Brown knew his team needed
to refocus for Game 2. He had
been in this position before.
Three years earlier, he was coach of the Philadelphia 76ers. His
team had reached the Finals and beaten the Lakers in Game 1
in Los Angeles. Then Brown watched Philadelphia get trounced
in the next four games. Brown worried it would happen again,
especially after the Lakers rallied to take Game 2 in overtime.

Ben Wallace, *right*, rises to block a shot attempt from the Lakers' Devean George during Game 5.

RIPPED APART

Game 3 moved the series to Detroit. The Pistons shook off the disappointing loss and came out firing. They started with an

8–0 run. Prince finished off a 24–16 first quarter by beating the buzzer with a three-pointer. For the rest of the game, Detroit leaned on Hamilton. The shooting guard finished with 31 points on 11-for-22 shooting. His counterpart, Bryant, was held in check. Guarded mostly by Prince, Bryant scored only one first-half point. When he finally woke up, it was too late. Detroit ran away with an 88–68 win.

Game 4 was tight for three quarters. But in the final 12 minutes, the Pistons took over. Rasheed Wallace, Hamilton, and Billups combined for 29 fourth-quarter points in an 88–80 victory. The Pistons now had a chance to clinch an unlikely title on their home floor.

Just a week earlier, everyone had been ready to crown Los Angeles as champions. Now TV announcer Al Michaels previewed Game 5 by saying, "The Lakers are lucky they haven't been swept."

Legendary singer Aretha Franklin had risen to fame in

Bill's Big Year

Pistons owner Bill Davidson achieved a first when the Pistons won the 2004 NBA title. Davidson was also the owner of the Tampa Bay Lightning of the National Hockey League. Just eight days before the Pistons' victory, the Lightning had defeated the Calgary Flames in the Stanley Cup Finals. Davidson was the first owner to ever hold both trophies at the same time. Davidson added a third championship when Detroit's Women's National Basketball Association team, the Shock, won that league's title in September 2004.

Detroit. She stunned the crowd with a rousing rendition of the national anthem before Game 5. The Pistons did the rest, taking it to the shattered Lakers starting in the second quarter. Hamilton, Ben Wallace, and reserve forward Mehmet Okur all chipped in seven points in the quarter as Detroit opened up a 10-point halftime lead. In the third, seven points from Prince guided the Pistons to a dominant 82–59 edge.

With 7:30 left, Hamilton missed a jumper from the baseline. But Ben Wallace rose above two Lakers, grabbed the ball with one hand, and slammed it home. As he hung on the rim for an extra second, Pistons fans partied in the stands. The celebration didn't stop until well after the final horn of a 100–87 Detroit win.

After it was over, Brown said of the unlikely winners, "I told them before the game, it would be a great statement if we had an opportunity to win, because we do play the right way, and we are truly a team."

Billups was named the Finals MVP. But he echoed Brown's thoughts in a post-game interview. "Everyone deserves this, not just me," Billups said. "I wish I could cut it into 13 pieces and give a little bit to everybody."

Chauncey Billups (1) holds up the NBA Finals MVP trophy after the Pistons knocked off the Lakers in five games.

ZOLLNER
12
PISTONS

CHAPTER TWO

PROUD HISTORY

The history of the Detroit Pistons didn't begin in Detroit. And it didn't begin in the NBA. The team played in the National Basketball League (NBL) from 1941 through 1948. At the time, the team played in Fort Wayne, Indiana. They were also called the "Zollner Pistons" after owner Fred Zollner. The owner also had a manufacturing business that made pistons for cars, trucks, and trains.

The Pistons won two league championships, in 1944 and 1945. In 1948 the Pistons left the NBL and joined the Basketball Association of America (BAA). Zollner also dropped his own name from the team's nickname. Just one year later, the BAA and NBL merged to form the 17-team NBA. The Fort Wayne Pistons were one of the first NBA teams.

The Pistons stayed in Fort Wayne through the NBA's first eight seasons. They reached the playoffs every year and made

George Yardley played seven seasons in the NBA and was an All-Star in six of them.

the NBA Finals for the first time in 1954–55. That team featured future Hall of Famers in guard Andy Phillip and forward George Yardley. But that was not enough to win a title as the Pistons lost in seven games to the Syracuse Nationals. A fourth Hall of Famer, forward Chuck Cooper, came on board the next year.

Another trip to the Finals came up short as the Pistons lost to the Philadelphia Warriors 4–1.

ON THE MOVE

Despite the success in Fort Wayne, Zollner wanted a bigger stage for the Pistons. In 1957 he moved the team to Detroit, which was then one of the largest cities in the United States. Detroit was already home to Major League Baseball's Tigers, the National Football League's Lions, and the National Hockey League's Red Wings.

"Professional basketball deserves a bigger audience than it has been getting in Fort Wayne," Zollner said. "I am convinced Detroit will support pro basketball just as it supports baseball, football, hockey, and the other pro sports."

Center Bob Lanier averaged 22.7 points per game in his 10 seasons with the Pistons.

The Pistons weren't as popular in Detroit as Zollner had hoped. They struggled to get fans to games in the early years. They struggled to win games too. But by the time the Pistons moved to Detroit, the NBA had shrunk to eight teams. Six made the playoffs. Because of that, the Pistons reached the playoffs in their first six seasons in their new home. However, they had losing records each time. Things got worse in the 1960s. When the Pistons finished 23–57 in 1963–64, they started a stretch of 10 miserable seasons. The team made the playoffs only once in that time.

FINALLY WINNERS

In 1970 Detroit drafted one of the greatest players in franchise history. Bob Lanier was a 6-foot-11-inch center from St. Bonaventure University. He was the big man Detroit needed to go with All-Star guards Dave Bing and Jimmy Walker. The trio led the Pistons to a 45–37 record in 1970–71. That was their first winning season in 15 years.

However, even that was not good enough to make the postseason. By 1970 the NBA had added nine new teams. It was not as easy to get into the playoffs. The Pistons were still on the outside looking in.

Detroit finally broke through in 1973–74. With Walker gone, Lanier and Bing led the Pistons to the playoffs. The stay was short, as the Pistons were beaten in the opening round by the Chicago Bulls. Detroit returned to the postseason each of the next three years but won only one round.

By then the team had a new owner. Zollner had sold the Pistons to local businessman Bill Davidson. Four years later, Davidson made a big move. He didn't like the Pistons' home gym, Cobo Arena. The Lions had recently built a huge stadium in the Detroit suburb of Pontiac, Michigan. It was called the Silverdome. Davidson decided his team would play there also.

The team that moved was one of the NBA's worst. In 1979–80 the Pistons finished 16–66. Even with their terrible

Head coach Chuck Daly, *right*, talks to star point guard Isiah Thomas.

record, it was still a landmark year in Pistons history. Davidson hired Jack McCloskey to be his general manager. No one knew it at the time, but the move would transform the Pistons.

BAD BOYS

Over the next decade, McCloskey aggressively rebuilt the roster. McCloskey's trades brought the team stars such as center Bill Laimbeer and guard Vinnie Johnson. Detroit also drafted well. Star point guard Isiah Thomas was taken second overall in 1981. Four years later, shooting guard Joe Dumars was picked eighteenth.

All the moves made Detroit a consistent playoff threat. Led by coach Chuck Daly, the Pistons started a nine-year playoff streak in 1983–84. But the Eastern Conference was dominated by the Boston Celtics in the 1980s. Detroit struggled to reach the Finals.

In 1988 Detroit's fortunes changed. The Pistons beat Boston in the Eastern Conference finals. They then went to the Finals and took the mighty Los Angeles Lakers to seven games before losing.

The Pistons took the final step the next year. They swept the Lakers in a Finals rematch. Detroit was finally an NBA champion. But not everyone was happy to see that.

The Pistons of the 1980s played a physical style of basketball. Players such as Laimbeer, power forward Rick Mahorn, and forward Dennis Rodman patrolled the lane. Anyone driving to the basket was in for a rough ride. Detroit fans loved it, but opponents did not. Many accused the Pistons of playing not just physical but dirty. The Pistons didn't care. They gave themselves the nickname "Bad Boys."

However they played, the Pistons were tough to beat. They repeated as champions in 1989–90. This time Detroit blew away the Portland Trail Blazers 4–1 in the Finals.

LONG ROAD TO A TITLE

In 1991 a new Eastern Conference dynasty had started with Michael Jordan's Chicago Bulls. Chicago beat the Pistons in the East finals that year. After that defeat, most of the Bad Boys

Owner Bill Davidson holds up the Larry O'Brien Trophy after point guard Isiah Thomas (11) and the Pistons won the team's first NBA title in 1989.

retired or moved on. Detroit sank back in the standings over the next decade.

By 2000 one of the Bad Boys was now in charge of running the Pistons. Former star Dumars was the team's new president. He was starting to assemble a roster of solid players.

It all came together in 2003–04. This Pistons won 54 games and reached the NBA Finals. Once there, they knocked off a Lakers team that featured two superstars in guard Kobe Bryant and center Shaquille O'Neal.

In a 4–1 Finals victory, three of Detroit's wins came by double digits. It was considered one of the biggest upsets in NBA history.

The Pistons remained one of the Eastern Conference's best teams for the next four seasons. They went as far as the conference finals each year. But their only other NBA Finals appearance came in 2005, when Detroit lost to the San Antonio Spurs in seven games.

TRYING TO REBUILD

By 2009–10 the Pistons were out of the playoffs again. As in the previous two decades, Detroit needed a new group of players to come together and make the team a winner. But Detroit had only one winning record and two playoff appearances in the 2010s.

Troy Weaver took over as the general manager after the 2019–20 season. Like McCloskey and Dumars, he started putting together a new roster. He drafted French point guard Killian Hayes seventh overall in the 2020 Draft. He also swung deals for the sixteenth pick, center Isaiah Stewart, and the eighteenth pick, small forward Saddiq Bey.

Pistons point guard Cade Cunningham, *center*, was named MVP of the Young Stars Game at the 2022 All-Star weekend.

In 2021 Detroit had the top pick. The Pistons used it on another guard, Cade Cunningham from Oklahoma State University. Suddenly the Pistons had a group of young, talented players ready to grow. The wins were still in short supply. But Detroit had hope around the corner.

CHAPTER THREE

DRIVING THE PISTONS

Fans of the modern NBA owe a lot to Fred Zollner. Without him, the league might not exist.

In 1949 professional basketball in the United States had two struggling leagues, the BAA and the NBL. Zollner knew something had to be done for basketball to survive. So, he called leaders from both leagues to a meeting at his house. Around his kitchen table, the two leagues hammered out a merger, and the NBA was born.

That was not Zollner's only contribution. He was a key figure in adding the 24-second shot clock that still exists today. He also advocated for widening the lane from 6 feet to 12 feet and for players to foul out after receiving six personal fouls.

Zollner sold the Pistons in 1974. A year later he was honored at the league's All-Star Game. Zollner was given the title of "Mr. Pro Basketball" for his contributions.

Pistons guard Dave Bing goes up for a jump shot during a 1968 game against the Philadelphia 76ers.

Zollner recruited several great players to Fort Wayne during the team's early years. None was better than small forward George Yardley. The slender, 6-foot-5-inch Yardley joined the team in 1953–54. He was soon one of the NBA's best scorers. The flashy Yardley made five All-Star teams, but his best season came in 1957–58. That year he made NBA history. On the final day of the NBA season, he had 26 points against the Syracuse Nationals. His final shot, a free throw, gave him 2,001 points for the year. No player had ever passed 2,000 points in an NBA season.

BOB AND BING

Pistons fans during the late 1960s didn't have much to cheer about. The team rarely made the playoffs. But that does not mean fans missed out on entertaining basketball.

In 1966 the Pistons had the second overall draft pick. They used it on point guard Dave Bing out of Syracuse University. He was an instant hit, averaging more than 20 points per game while winning Rookie of the Year honors. A year later, Detroit had the top pick. They grabbed another guard, Jimmy Walker, from Providence College. Walker made the All-Star team twice with the Pistons.

When Walker and Bing weren't scoring outside, they moved the ball inside to Bob Lanier. The towering 6-foot-11-inch center was also a number one pick, in 1970. For the next decade he piled up points in Detroit. When he finally left the team in 1980, Lanier was the Pistons' all-time leading scorer.

Dave DeBusschere might be best known for his years with the New York Knicks, but he was a great Piston as well. The 6-foot-6-inch forward played seven seasons in Detroit and was a three-time All-Star. For three of his playing years, 1964–65 to 1966–67, he was also the Pistons' head coach. At 24 years old, he was the youngest head coach in NBA history. It was not a very successful run. Detroit went just 79–143 with DeBusschere leading the way.

THE BAD BOYS

When Jack McCloskey took over the Detroit Pistons in 1979, he had a huge job. The team didn't have much talent. McCloskey went to work fixing that by making trades—a lot of them. By the time he had turned the Pistons into NBA champions

10 years later, "Trader Jack" had made nearly 30 deals. And along the way, he had hired a game-changing coach in Chuck Daly.

The strategy worked. One of McCloskey's first big moves was to bring in guard Vinnie Johnson in 1981. Johnson wasn't playing much for the Seattle SuperSonics. In 10 seasons with the Pistons, Johnson became a key bench scorer. He earned the nickname "the Microwave" for his ability to get hot quickly as a shooter.

Three months later McCloskey made a multiplayer deal with the Cleveland Cavaliers. Detroit picked up center Bill Laimbeer. The rugged 6-foot-11-inch Laimbeer was never Detroit's key scorer. His biggest contributions came at the other end of the floor. As the Pistons developed a reputation as the NBA's toughest team, Laimbeer was the ringleader. He was known for his hard fouls. But Laimbeer was a solid scorer and one of the game's best rebounders as well. With Laimbeer, Rick Mahorn, and a young, skinny rebounder named Dennis Rodman, the Pistons were a force in the paint.

While Laimbeer provided the brawn inside, point guard Isiah Thomas was the brains of the Pistons—and the flash. Drafted in 1981 out of Indiana University, Thomas started Detroit's climb to a championship the minute he stepped on his first NBA court. By the time Detroit made it back to

Dennis Rodman (10) was one of the "Bad Boys" that made Detroit such a tough opponent in the late 1980s and early 1990s.

the playoffs in 1983–84, Thomas was averaging more than 20 points and 11 assists per game.

Thomas was a combination of slick passes and fearless drives to the basket. He was undersized at 6 feet, 1 inch and 180 pounds, but few players were tougher. He showed that during the 1988 NBA Finals. With the Pistons facing the Lakers in Game 6, Thomas scored 25 points in the third quarter alone. He had already scored 14 when he rolled his ankle. Limping badly, he returned to the court and scored 11 more

Point guard Isiah Thomas, *center*, and center Bill Laimbeer, *right*, formed the backbone of the Pistons' championship teams in 1989 and 1990.

points. It was a sign of the competitiveness that both he and Laimbeer shared.

"Hated to lose. That's the one thing they both had in common. Both of them hated to lose," Johnson said of his teammates.

The Pistons didn't lose much after they added shooting guard Joe Dumars in 1985. An excellent shooter, Dumars was the perfect complement to Thomas in the backcourt. He was the Most Valuable Player (MVP) of the NBA Finals when the Pistons finally broke through in 1989. Dumars averaged 27.3 points per game during the four-game sweep of the Lakers.

Meanwhile, bringing it all together was Daly. When he was hired in 1983, the Pistons had not had two straight winning seasons since they played in Fort Wayne. Daly put a winner on the floor for nine straight years before leaving the team in 1992. Affectionately known as "Daddy Rich" by his players for his fancy clothes, Daly continually got the best out of his teams. The Detroit Pistons of the 1980s had many strong personalities, but Daly was able to bring them all together.

GOIN' TO WORK

Dumars spent his entire career with the Pistons before retiring in 1999. Within a year, he was the team's president of basketball operations. During the 1990s the Pistons had relied on stars like forward Grant Hill and guard Jerry Stackhouse. But the team did not win enough.

Dumars started grabbing up solid veteran players. Point guard Chauncey Billups was an NBA journeyman when he signed with the Pistons in July 2002. But he was still only 26. He teamed up in the backcourt with 24-year-old scorer Richard "Rip" Hamilton, who came over in a trade from the Washington Wizards two months later.

Ben Wallace was considered small for a center at 6 feet, 9 inches and 240 pounds. He hadn't played much when he joined the Pistons in 2000. The fiercely competitive Wallace wasn't a great scorer, but he was one of the league's best rebounders and shot blockers from the moment he arrived in Detroit. By the time he left the Pistons in 2006, he was a four-time All-Star. He later rejoined Detroit for the final three years of his career before retiring in 2012.

Ben Wallace (3) led the NBA in rebounding twice while wearing a Pistons uniform.

Rasheed Wallace was not related to Ben, but he shared the same competitive drive. The smooth-shooting big man had been a star for the Portland Trail Blazers, but he was known to go over the line. Wallace received an NBA-record 41 technical fouls during the 2000–01 season.

That didn't scare the Pistons away from trading for him late in the 2003–04 season. Rasheed Wallace proved the final piece of the puzzle as Detroit trounced the Los Angeles Lakers in that year's NBA Finals.

That group led the Pistons to six consecutive Eastern Conference finals from 2003 to 2008. While none of the players were superstars, Detroit had the perfect group. The team even had a nickname that proved they weren't flashy. They were called the "Goin' to Work" Pistons.

A NEW DAY

On the heels of one of its worst seasons ever in 2020–21, Detroit needed a new star. The Pistons felt confident they had found one in point guard Cade Cunningham. The 6-foot-5-inch point guard could score, pass, and rebound. It took him only 11 games to record his first NBA triple-double. The league took notice of him right away.

"I think Cade is going to be a special player in this league," said Billups, who became the head coach of the Trail Blazers in 2021–22. "He's a special talent. He can do everything you ask out there."

With young talent like Cunningham, guard Killian Hayes, forward Saddiq Bey, and center Isaiah Stewart, the Pistons hoped they had the core of their next championship team already in place.

Point guard Cade Cunningham poses with his Pistons jersey after the team took him with the top selection in the 2021 NBA Draft.

ZOLLNER
9
PISTONS
HAWKS
9

CHAPTER FOUR

PISTON POWER

Pistons fans have celebrated three titles in Detroit. But fans who watched the team in Fort Wayne remember the one that got away in 1954–55. That year the Pistons finished 43–29. This record would stand as the best winning percentage in team history for nearly three decades.

Facing the Syracuse Nationals in the NBA Finals, the Pistons fell behind 2–0. Fort Wayne then captured the next three games before Syracuse won Game 6.

The final game came down to the last second. Fort Wayne had let a 17-point first-half lead slip away but had the ball with the game tied 91–91. However, forward George Yardley was called for palming the basketball. After the turnover, Fort Wayne guard Frankie Brian fouled the Nationals' George King. The point guard sank a free throw to put Syracuse ahead.

Fort Wayne power forward Mel Hutchins, *left*, goes up for a layup against the St. Louis Hawks during the 1956 playoffs.

With one possession left, the Pistons gave the ball to point guard Andy Phillip. But King stole the ball from Phillip before Fort Wayne could ever get a shot away. The Nationals held on for the 92–91 win.

BACK TO BACK

The Pistons were a long-suffering franchise before they finally broke through in the late 1980s. In Game 7 of the 1974 playoffs, another late steal cost the Pistons a series win against the Chicago Bulls. It happened again in Game 5 of the 1987 Eastern Conference finals against the Boston Celtics. Larry Bird stole an inbounds pass and fed Dennis Johnson for a layup that beat the Pistons. Boston ended up winning the series.

In 1988 the Pistons reached the NBA Finals. They even led the Los Angeles Lakers 102–101 with 27 seconds left in Game 6. Detroit needed one stop to clinch a title. But Bill Laimbeer

Joe Dumars, *center*, and the Pistons had a fierce rivalry with the Boston Celtics during the 1980s.

was called for a foul on Lakers center Kareem Abdul-Jabbar. The superstar sank two free throws as the Lakers went on to win both that game and Game 7. Lakers coach Pat Riley later admitted the officials got the call wrong.

Detroit was back in 1989. This time the Pistons left no doubt. They upended the Lakers in four games. Three of the games were close into the final minute, but Detroit's defense kept the Lakers off balance enough to pull through.

Detroit then faced the Portland Trail Blazers in the 1990 NBA Finals. The Pistons took a 3–1 lead into Game 5 in Portland. But the Trail Blazers had kept the games close all series and led 90–83 with 2:02 remaining. Detroit then turned on "the Microwave." Reserve guard Vinnie Johnson scored seven of his 16 points in the final minutes.

With 16 seconds left, the Pistons had the ball in a 90–90 tie. Isiah Thomas passed off to Johnson on the right wing. Johnson first tried to back down

Vinnie Johnson's offense off the bench was a key factor for the Pistons during his 10 years with the team.

defender Jerome Kersey. But suddenly the Pistons guard changed his mind and pulled up from 15 feet. Johnson's shot dropped in with 0.7 seconds left on the clock. The Pistons were champions again. With that shot, Detroit became just the third team in NBA history to win back-to-back titles, joining the Celtics and the Lakers.

PUTTING THE "D" IN DETROIT

Before the Pistons could shock the world in the 2004 NBA Finals, they had to get past the New Jersey Nets. The Nets were the two-time defending Eastern conference champions. A year earlier, they had crushed a favored Detroit team in the East finals, winning in four games.

The teams met again in the 2004 second round. Detroit got off to a fast start with two lopsided victories. But New Jersey bounced back to rout the Pistons in Games 3 and 4. A miracle half-court three-pointer at the buzzer by Detroit point guard Chauncey Billups in Game 5 sent the game into overtime. But then Detroit started to run

Forward Rasheed Wallace averaged 13.0 points and 7.8 rebounds during the Pistons' championship run in the 2004 playoffs.

out of gas—and players. As the game stretched into the third overtime, Ben Wallace, Rasheed Wallace, and Richard Hamilton had all fouled out. Tayshaun Prince committed his sixth foul with one second left in the game. New Jersey's 127–120 triple-overtime win ended with four of Detroit's five starters on the bench.

After three losses in a row, Pistons fans feared the series was over. It looked worse when New Jersey jumped to a 13–2 lead in Game 6. It was another chance for the gritty Pistons to show their mental strength. Detroit turned the tide and outscored New Jersey 48–23 over the rest of the first half. The game tightened back up in the second, but the Pistons held on for an 81–75 win.

That set up a dramatic Game 7 back in Detroit. All year, the Pistons had beaten teams by smothering them defensively. With the series on the line, they did it again. Their toughness held the Nets to 31 first-half points. And in the third quarter, Detroit put the series away. Billups and center Ben Wallace each scored 10 points. The Nets, on the other hand, couldn't get a good look. They shot just 4-for-15 in the quarter.

The final score was 90–69. It was the thirteenth time that season the Pistons had held a team below 70 points in a game. Detroit would do that four more times in the next two playoff rounds on its way to an NBA title.

LEAVING NO DOUBT

The Pistons entered the 2018–19 season with only one playoff appearance in the previous nine years. After a hot 13-7 start, fans started to wonder if they might get back in the postseason.

The Pistons then started to nosedive. They went 4–11 in December. In January they went 6–10. Detroit played better over the final two months but still needed to win its last two games to make the playoffs.

On April 9 the Pistons knocked off the Memphis Grizzlies 100–93 to stay alive. Detroit entered the season's final day with a record of 40–41. Detroit would have to win on the road at the struggling Knicks to clinch a spot.

Led by center Andre Drummond, guard Reggie Jackson, and reserve Luke Kennard, the Pistons blitzed New York in the first half. Kennard led the way with 19 points. When Drummond slammed home a dunk with 20 seconds left in the second quarter, Detroit led 65–41.

Detroit never let the Knicks up in a 115–89 victory. Kennard finished with a game-high 27 points. Detroit's playoff stay was short, as the Milwaukee Bucks swept the Pistons in the first round. But with young stars on the way, Detroit hoped to have more postseason memories soon.

Pistons center Andre Drummond throws up a hook shot during the Pistons' playoff-clinching rout over the New York Knicks in April 2019.

TIMELINE

1941

The Fort Wayne Zollner Pistons, owned by Fred Zollner, begin play in the National Basketball League. They go on to play in the NBL through 1948 before joining the Basketball Association of America.

1949

The NBL and BAA merge to form the NBA. The Fort Wayne Pistons are one of the first teams.

1955

The Pistons reach the NBA Finals for the first time but fall in seven games to the Syracuse Nationals.

1957

After 16 years in Fort Wayne, Zollner moves the Pistons to Detroit.

1970

The Pistons select Bob Lanier with the top pick in the NBA Draft. In 10 seasons with the team, Lanier sets a franchise record by scoring 15,488 points while helping Detroit reach the playoffs four times.

1974

Zollner sells the team to Detroit businessman Bill Davidson.

1979

Davidson hires Jack McCloskey as the Pistons' general manager.

1981

McCloskey drafts point guard Isiah Thomas second overall in the NBA Draft, beginning Thomas's Hall-of-Fame career in Detroit.

1989

Led by Thomas, coach Chuck Daly, and the "Bad Boys," the Pistons win the first NBA title in team history by sweeping the Los Angeles Lakers.

1990

The Pistons repeat as champions by beating the Portland Trail Blazers 4–1.

2000

A year after retiring as a player, Joe Dumars is hired as the president of basketball operations for the Pistons.

2004

Behind Finals MVP Chauncey Billups, the Pistons defeat the Los Angeles Lakers 4–1 to win their third NBA title.

2009

The Pistons lose in the first round of the playoffs, ending a streak of six consecutive Eastern Conference finals appearances.

2019

The Pistons rout the New York Knicks on the final day of the regular season to reach the NBA playoffs for just the second time in 10 years.

2021

The Pistons select point guard Cade Cunningham from Oklahoma State University with the first pick in the NBA Draft.

FRANCHISE HISTORY

Fort Wayne Zollner Pistons (1941–1948)
Fort Wayne Pistons (1948–1957)
Detroit Pistons (1957–)

NBA CHAMPIONSHIPS

1989, 1990, 2004

KEY PLAYERS

Chauncey Billups (2002–08)
Dave Bing (1966–75)
Cade Cunningham (2021–)
Dave DeBusschere (1962–68)
Andre Drummond (2012–20)
Joe Dumars (1985–99)
Larry Foust (1950–57)
Richard Hamilton (2002–11)
Grant Hill (1994–2000)
Bill Laimbeer (1982–93)
Bob Lanier (1970–80)
Isiah Thomas (1981–94)
Ben Wallace (2000–06, 2009–12)
Rasheed Wallace (2004–09)
George Yardley (1953–59)

KEY COACHES

Larry Brown (2003–05)
Chuck Daly (1983–92)

HOME ARENAS

North Side High School Gym (1948–52)
War Memorial Coliseum (1952–57)
Olympia Stadium (1957–61)
Cobo Arena (1961–78)
Pontiac Silverdome (1978–88)
The Palace of Auburn Hills (1988–2017)
Little Caesars Arena (2017–)

TWO-SPORT STAR

In 1952 the Fort Wayne Pistons selected Duke University star Dick Groat with the third overall pick in the NBA Draft. Groat played only one season in the NBA before turning to baseball. He played 14 seasons of Major League Baseball and won the 1960 National League MVP Award.

THE GOOD GUY

Despite playing for the "Bad Boys" Pistons, Joe Dumars won the NBA's first Sportsmanship Award in 1996. The award is now known as the Joe Dumars Trophy.

ONE OF A KIND

Larry Brown stands alone in the world of basketball coaches. He had already won a college championship with Kansas University in 1988. After winning the NBA title with the Pistons in 2004, he became the only coach ever to have won both.

FILLING UP THE SILVER DOME

Detroit played in the Pontiac Silverdome from 1978 to 1988. The 82,000-seat stadium was normally home to football's Detroit Lions. That led to some of the largest crowds in NBA history for Pistons games. On January 29, 1988, a crowd of 61,983 fans watched the Pistons beat the Boston Celtics 125–108. That set an NBA attendance record that stood for 10 years.

GLOSSARY

assist
A pass that leads directly to a basket.

draft
A system that allows teams to acquire new players coming into a league.

franchise
A sports organization, including the top-level team and all minor league affiliates.

palming
Also called carrying, a violation that occurs when a player puts his hand underneath the basketball while dribbling.

postseason
Another word for playoffs; the time after the end of the regular season when teams play to determine a champion.

rebound
To catch the ball after a shot has been missed.

rookie
A professional athlete in his or her first year of competition.

roster
A list of players who make up a team.

steal
To take the ball from a player on the other team.

triple-double
Accumulating 10 or more of three certain statistics in a game.

veteran
A player who has played for many years.

MORE
INFORMATION

BOOKS

Flynn, Brendan. *The NBA Encyclopedia for Kids*. Minneapolis, MN: Abdo Publishing, 2022.

Mahoney, Brian. *GOATs of Basketball*. Minneapolis, MN: Abdo Publishing, 2022.

Ybarra, Andres. *Great Basketball Debates*. Minneapolis, MN: Abdo Publishing, 2019.

ONLINE RESOURCES

To learn more about the Detroit Pistons, please visit **abdobooklinks.com** or scan this QR code. These links are routinely monitored and updated to provide the most current information available.

ABOUT THE AUTHOR

Brian Howell has been an author and sports journalist for more than 28 years. He has written several books about sports and covered major events such as the US Open golf tournament, the World Series, the Stanley Cup Playoffs, the NBA All-Star Game, and playoff games in the NBA and NFL. He has earned several writing awards during his career. The Colorado native lives with his wife and four children.